To renew this book, phone 0845 1202811 or visit
our website at www.libcat.oxfordshire.gov.uk
You will need your library PIN number
(available from your library)

**OXFORDSHIRE
COUNTY COUNCIL**
SOCIAL & COMMUNITY SERVICES
www.oxfordshire.gov.uk

TOXIC TERROR!

BY
ROBIN TWIDDY

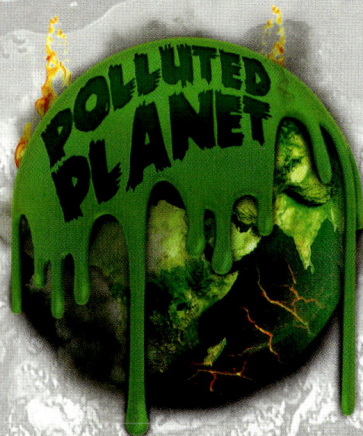

POLLUTED PLANET

BookLife
PUBLISHING

©2019
BookLife Publishing
King's Lynn
Norfolk, PE30 4LS

Written by:
Robin Twiddy

Edited by:
Kirsty Holmes

Designed by:
Drue Rintoul

All facts, statistics, web addresses
and URLs in this book were verified
as valid and accurate at time of writing.

No responsibility for any changes
to external websites or references
can be accepted by either the author
or publisher.

PHOTO CREDITS

CONTENTS

Words that look like **this** are explained in the glossary on page 31.

LET ME TELL YOU A STORY...

Welcome, welcome. Please take a seat and let me tell you a story. A tale of human horror and toxic terror, of a world on the brink of destruction, of the **nefarious** beings who planned the end of the world... and the one girl who could stop them.

High above this globe we call home, a plot was being revealed. An alien species with designs for the Earth prepared to bring their plan to its conclusion.

FINALLY, AFTER DECADES OF GUIDING MANKIND AND PULLING THEIR STRINGS WITH OUR SLIMY TENTACLES, THE EARTH IS ALMOST READY FOR THE TAKING.

AND THEY SAID WE COULDN'T DO IT: CONVINCE HUMANITY TO MAKE THEIR OWN WORLD COMPLETELY **UNINHABITABLE** FOR EARTHLINGS. *BLUUURP!* HA HA HA HA HA HA HA!

FRAXULON, TAKE US INTO EARTH'S ORBIT. WE MUST CHECK OUR PROGRESS. WE NEED AIR, SOIL AND WATER SAMPLES TO TEST THE TOXICITY LEVELS.

AS YOU COMMAND... *BLUURRP...* COMMANDER ZURP!

Fraxulon initiated the second-stage turbine and the strange metallic vehicle zoomed at an impossible speed towards the Earth. Breaking through the atmosphere, it headed towards a small town in the UK.

UNIVERSAL TRANSLATOR

INITIATED

SAY

IN-ISH-EE-ATE-ED

MEANING

TO START OR BEGIN

5

MEANWHILE, ON EARTH...

Meanwhile, in a small town on Earth, a young girl by the name of Angelina Butterworth was recycling used batteries collected from her school, when she came across a strange sight in the sky!

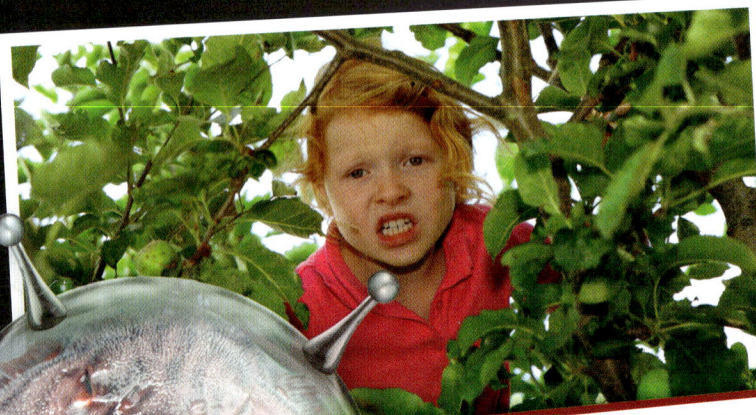

Angelina followed the strange object to where it eventually landed. Here, she watched as an incredible sight unfolded from the bushes.

RELEASE THE TRI-MONO MONITOR!

AS YOU WISH, COMMANDER.

BLEEP

BLOOP

Young Angelina looked on, frozen in horror, as the strange alien creatures released an even stranger device that began to bleep, bloop and whoop.

WHOOP

THE TRI-MONO MONITOR HAS FINISHED SCANNING, COMMANDER ZURP!

TOXICITY CONVERSION

WATER: 68%

AIR: 73%

SOIL: 69%

Now, reader: what would you do if you saw two gross, burbling aliens up to no good in your local park? Well, I couldn't say what Angelina wanted to do, but I can tell you what she actually did. She SCREAMED!

Tractor Beam

Angelina grabbed her bike and tried to escape. But alien spacecraft are faster than pedal bikes, and she was soon caught in the alien tractor beam.

ABDUCTED!

Trapped inside some sort of energy field, Angelina was confronted by her captors.

WHO ARE YOU? WHAT DO YOU WANT WITH ME? WHAT WAS THAT THING THAT WAS ALL BLOOPY AND BLEEPY? AND WHY DO YOU LOOK LIKE THAT?

Like any good villain in a bad movie, Zurp and Fraxulon began to explain their villainous plan.

WE ARE TOXLINGS FROM THE PLANET TOXONIA: A BEAUTIFUL WORLD FULL OF TOXIC SWAMPS, FIZZING CHEMICAL SLUDGE AND ACID RAIN. OH, HOW I MISS THE ACID RAIN.

WE WERE SENT TO EARTH NEARLY 200 YEARS AGO TO PREPARE YOUR WORLD FOR THE GREAT INVASION. YOU SEE, YOUR PLANET WAS TOO CLEAN AND TOO PURE FOR TOXLINGS. OUR MISSION WAS TO SLOWLY POLLUTE YOUR PLANET, TO MAKE IT MORE LIKE OURS.

SOON, OUR MISSION WILL BE COMPLETE. YOUR WORLD WILL BECOME LIKE OURS: A TOXIC WORLD OF DELICIOUS POLLUTION, AIR THICK WITH SMOG, WATER THAT SIZZLES AND BUBBLES AND SOIL THAT BURNS TO THE TOUCH.

BUT, WE ARE SO CLOSE TO COMPLETING OUR MISSION ... *GLUUUUURBLE* ... WE CAN'T LET ANYONE REVEAL OUR PRESENCE AND THREATEN *THE GRAND PLAN*.

IT DIDN'T TAKE LONG TO **EXPLOIT** HUMANITY'S GREED AND CONVINCE YOU STUPID HUMANS TO START POLLUTING YOUR OWN WORLD. WITH A FEW NUDGES ... *UURGHRUP* ... YOUR PEOPLE HAVE DONE MOST OF OUR WORK FOR US.

TOXIC TERRAFORMING

WHEN WE FIRST ARRIVED, THE HUMAN RACE WAS JUST BEGINNING TO BUILD FACTORIES. THEY CALLED IT THE **INDUSTRIAL REVOLUTION**. WE CALLED IT OUR WAY IN.

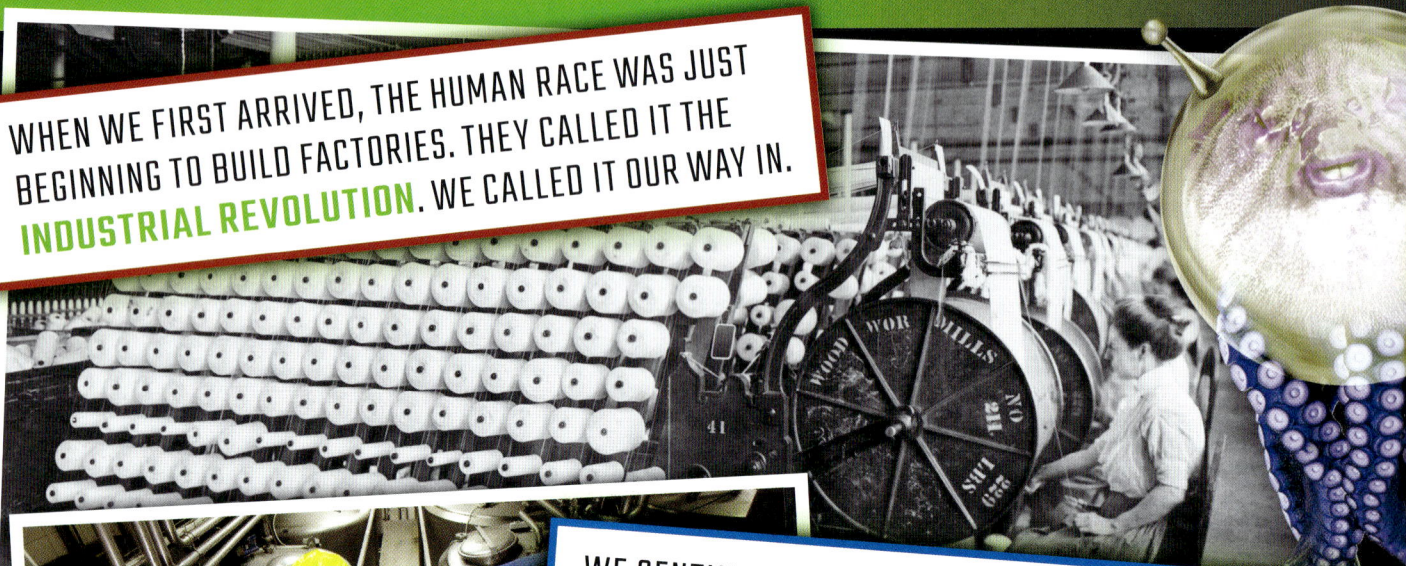

WE GENTLY GUIDED THESE FACTORY OWNERS TOWARDS MAKING MORE **SYNTHETIC** AND DANGEROUS PRODUCTS. WE KNEW THAT IT WOULD BE YEARS BEFORE ANYONE REALISED THE HARM THEY WERE DOING.

BUT PEOPLE AREN'T STUPID ENOUGH TO LISTEN TO YOU TWO – EVEN BACK THEN! HOW DID YOU DO IT?

IT WAS SIMPLE REALLY. JUST A MATTER OF LEAVING THE RIGHT THINGS WHERE THE RIGHT PEOPLE WOULD FIND THEM. A FORMULA HERE, A PIECE OF PLASTIC THERE. GREEDY PEOPLE ARE EASY TO CONTROL.

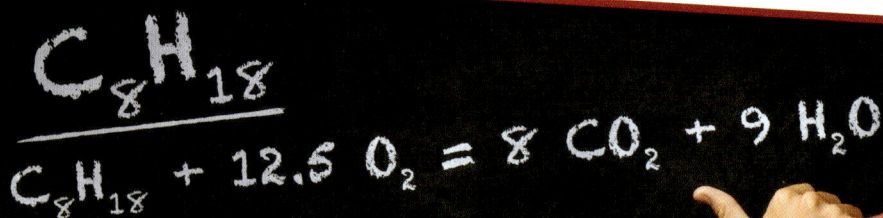

$$\frac{C_8H_{18}}{C_8H_{18} + 12.5\,O_2 = 8\,CO_2 + 9\,H_2O}$$

PETROL FORMULA

WE DID A LOT OF OUR BEST WORK DURING, AND JUST AFTER, THE SECOND WORLD WAR. BOTH SIDES WOULD HAVE USED ANYTHING TO WIN THAT WAR AND WE WERE HAPPY TO GIVE THEM THE THINGS THEY NEEDED.

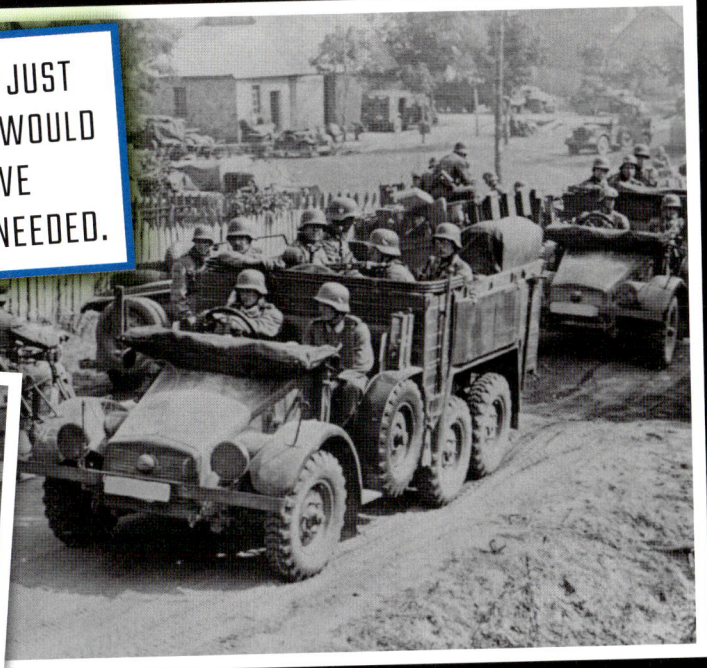

This war led to huge scientific discoveries and a large increase in **manufacturing**. As the needs of the war increased, so too did the demands on the factories.

NEW WAYS TO MANUFACTURE MEANT NEW WAYS TO POLLUTE.

DON'T FORGET THE BOMBINGS... *URRRRP*! THEY CAUSED SO MUCH DAMAGE!

AH YES, THE BOMBINGS. MANY OIL REFINERIES WERE BOMBED DURING THE SECOND WORLD WAR. LOTS OF CHEMICAL WEAPONS WERE LEFT OVER FROM THE WAR. SOME, SUCH AS MUSTARD GAS, ARE STILL THREATENING EARTH'S ENVIRONMENT OVER 75 YEARS LATER!

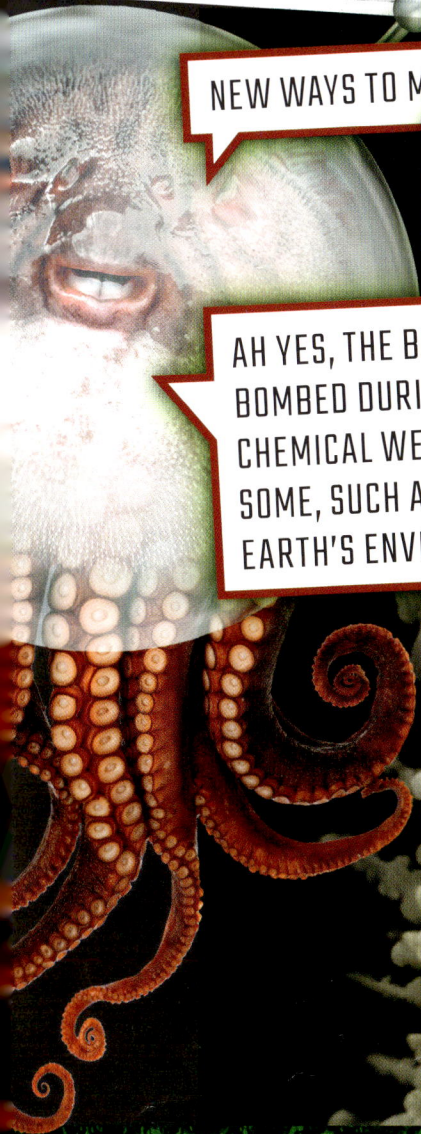

MEN IN BLACK

In the 1950s and 1960s there were multiple sightings of 'men in black' – mysterious men who appeared *almost* human.

WE **INFILTRATED** THE GOVERNMENTS OF THE WORLD WITH OUR MEN IN BLACK. THEY DIRECTED THE GOVERNMENTS TO MAKE MANUFACTURING MORE AND MORE TOXIC.

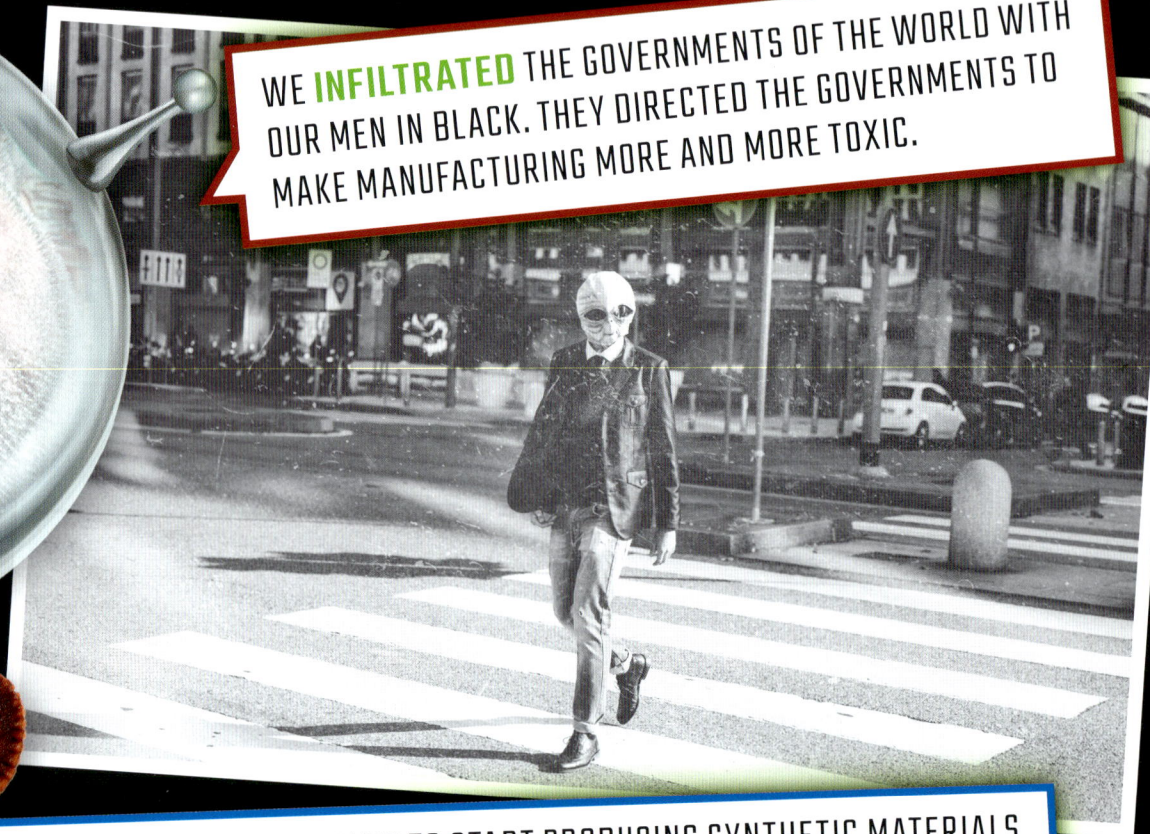

THE TRICK WAS TO CONVINCE GOVERNMENTS TO START PRODUCING SYNTHETIC MATERIALS.

Synthetic materials, such as plastic, are not found in nature. They often do not **biodegrade** in the same way that natural materials do. In fact, many actually release toxins as they breakdown.

OUR GREATEST TRICK WAS TO CONVINCE HUMANITY THAT IT COULD CREATE A SOLUTION TO ANY PROBLEM IN A LABORATORY.

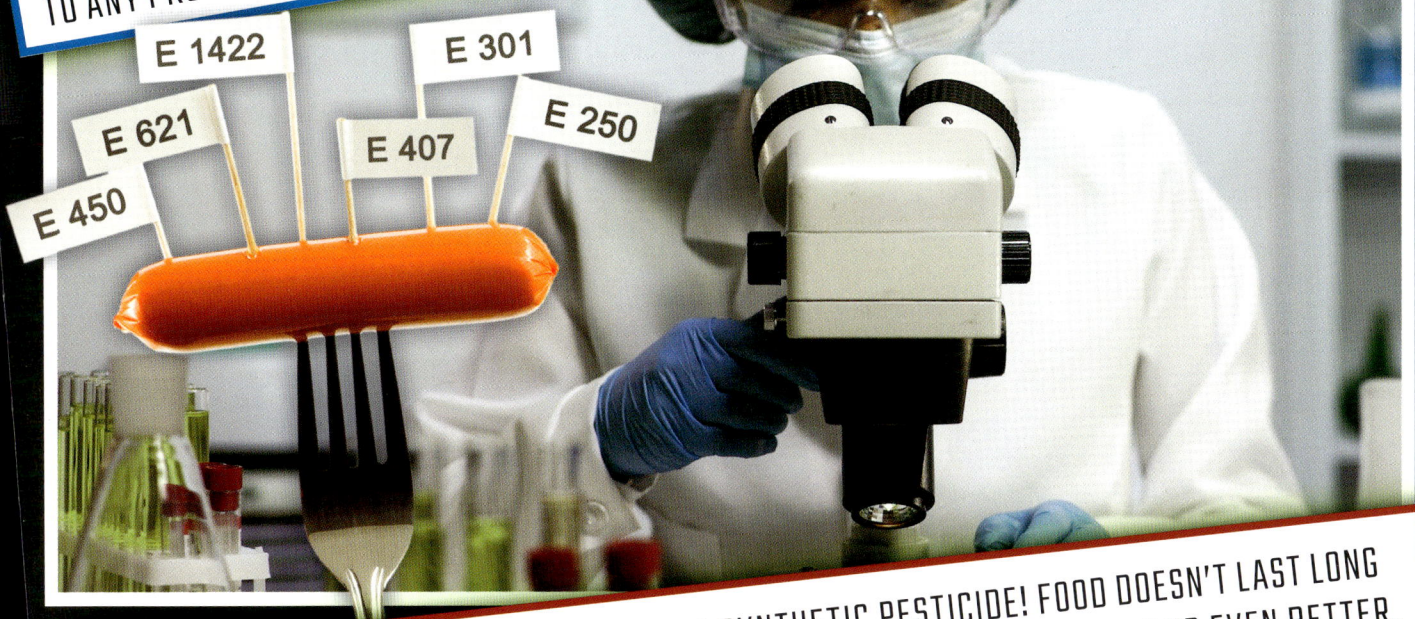

E 1422

E 301

E 621

E 407

E 250

E 450

TOO MANY INSECTS ON YOUR CROPS? MAKE A SYNTHETIC PESTICIDE! FOOD DOESN'T LAST LONG ENOUGH? WHY NOT ADD SOMETHING THAT WILL SLOW THE ROTTING PROCESS? OR EVEN BETTER, WHY NOT SEAL IT IN PLASTIC?

The Toxlings were masters of **psychology**, **manipulating** the human race with ease. In no time at all, people were finding solutions to problems that did not even exist, such as the shoe umbrella or chewing gum. If people were hungry, why didn't they just eat?

AH, YES, IT WAS DURING THIS TIME THAT WE ENCOURAGED THE USE OF PLASTIC. FOOLISH HUMANS; YOU BELIEVED THAT THIS NEW MATERIAL WOULD LEAD TO A BETTER WORLD. WELL, IT DID – JUST NOT FOR YOU! MWAH-HA-HA-HAA!

PLEASE SIR, CAN I HAVE SOME MORE...
PLASTIC?

OH, YOU LITTLE HUMANS COULDN'T GET ENOUGH OF THAT PLASTIC. THINK ABOUT HOW MUCH ... *BELCH*... PLASTIC YOU SEE AND TOUCH EVERY DAY. LOTS, I WOULD BET!

PLASTIC

PLASTIC

PLASTIC

PLASTIC

PLASTIC

PLASTIC

PLASTIC

PLASTIC IS PERFECT! MAKING IT PRODUCES TOXIC WASTE, MELTING IT PRODUCES TOXIC WASTE, AND LETTING IT SIT IN WATER RELEASES TOXIC CHEMICALS.

THE PLASTIC WORKED BETTER THAN WE EXPECTED. IT CAN BE FOUND ANYWHERE YOU LOOK NOW. THE OCEANS, THE LAND, INSIDE ANIMALS AND EVEN IN THE HUMAN BODY. ALMOST EVERY PERSON ON THE PLANET IS NOW INFECTED WITH PLASTIC. IT CAN BE FOUND IN THE URINE AND BLOOD OF ALMOST EVERY PERSON ON THE PLANET.

IS THAT MY BLOOD?

AND THE BEST DRESSED PEST AWARD GOES TO...
HUMANITY!

SPEAKING OF PESTS, IT WAS A REALLY GOOD IDEA FOR YOU PEOPLE TO START COVERING YOUR OWN FOOD WITH POISON JUST TO GET RID OF THEM. OH WE HAD A GOOD LAUGH AT YOU WHEN YOU STARTED USING PESTICIDES!

DON'T FORGET DDT. IT WAS USED TO GET RID OF INSECTS BUT IT WAS SO BAD THAT THEY BANNED IT IN THE USA. EVEN NOW, OVER 40 YEARS LATER, WE CAN STILL FIND TRACES OF IT IN 99% OF PEOPLE, IN 60% OF HEAVY CREAMS AND 28% OF CARROTS IN THE UNITED STATES.

DDT was a disaster for America. This synthetic pesticide almost led to the extinction of the bald eagle, girls exposed to it before **puberty** were five times more likely to suffer from breast cancer, and it still lingers in the soil, just as the Toxlings planned.

UNIVERSAL TRANSLATOR

DDT
DICHLORODIPHENYLTRICHLORDETHANE

TAKE A DEEP BREATH AND SAY
DIE-KLOR-O-DIE-FEN-UL-TRY-KLOR-O-ETH-AYNE

15

RISE OF THE
TOXIC TOYS!

DO YOU LIKE YOUR COMPUTER? YOUR TABLET? HOW ABOUT YOUR GAMES CONSOLE? OR YOUR PHONE? OH YOU DO? WELL, SO DO WE. EACH OF THOSE DEVICES HAS LITTLE TOXIC PARTS. WHAT DO YOU KNOW ABOUT HEAVY METALS?

Angelina thought about the music her dad listened to. 'Yes,' she thought. 'That is pretty toxic.' She certainly didn't like it, or the way her dad danced to it, but maybe this wasn't the type of heavy metal Fraxulon was talking about...

SOME OF THE MOST TOXIC THINGS ON THIS PLANET ARE HEAVY METALS; YOU STUPID HUMANS ARE PUTTING THEM IN EVERYTHING... *BLURP*!!!

Zurp fired up a display screen.

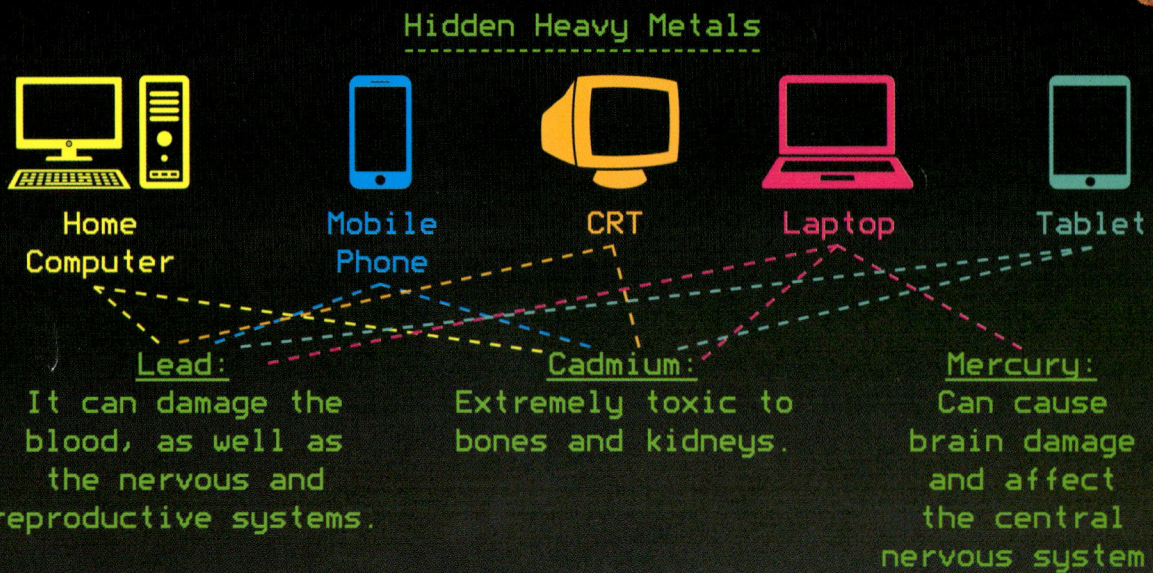

Hidden Heavy Metals

Home Computer   Mobile Phone   CRT   Laptop   Tablet

Lead:
It can damage the blood, as well as the nervous and reproductive systems.

Cadmium:
Extremely toxic to bones and kidneys.

Mercury:
Can cause brain damage and affect the central nervous system.

WHAT DO YOU THINK HAPPENS TO ALL THAT ELECTRONIC WASTE? YOU THROW IT OUT AND IT'S GONE? NO! IT GOES TO **LANDFILLS** OR IS SENT ...*BLURP*... TO NATIONS WITH **DEVELOPING ECONOMIES**. ONCE THERE, THOSE PRECIOUS TOXIC HEAVY METALS BEGIN TO **LEACH** INTO THE ENVIRONMENT.

Things used to be built to last for a long time. People were proud of their ability to mend and fix things, keeping stuff in good condition so they would last longer. Manufacturers would advertise their products as being 'built for life'. So how did the Toxlings persuade them to move to cheap throwaway products? Greed, dear reader: the answer is greed.

FRAXULON HAD AN EXCELLENT IDEA: HE INTRODUCED THE HUMANS TO THE IDEA OF PLANNED **OBSOLESCENCE**. THIS MEANS THAT AN ELECTRONIC DEVICE IS DESIGNED TO BREAK OR BECOME TOO OLD TO USE, AND HOW LONG IT LASTS BEFORE YOU NEED A NEW ONE IS DECIDED BY THE MANUFACTURER. THIS MEANT THAT PEOPLE THREW AWAY OLD ELECTRONICS INSTEAD OF HAVING THEM FIXED, LEAVING MORE TOXIC TRASH.

CLEANING KILLS!

HAVE YOU EVER WONDERED WHY SO MANY CLEANING PRODUCTS IN YOUR HOUSE SAY THINGS SUCH AS 'HAZARDOUS TO HUMANS AND DOMESTIC ANIMALS'? WE DID THAT.

In the early **21st century**, the average home had around 62 toxic chemicals in it. What clever villains the Toxlings are, making cleanliness toxic!

MOST OF THESE CHEMICALS ARE HARMLESS IN SMALL DOSES, SUCH AS WHEN YOU USE THEM TO CLEAN WITH, BUT THE BODY CAN STORE THESE TOXINS.

I PRIDE MYSELF ON MY ABILITY TO GATHER TOXINS IN MY BODY. DID YOU KNOW I CAN RELEASE THEM AS A GAS?

UNIVERSAL TRANSLATOR

PERCHLOROETHYLENE
SAY
PER-KLO-RO-EF-E-LENE

QUATERNARY AMMONIUM COMPOUNDS
SAY
KWOT-ER-NER-EE AMM-OH-NEE-UM COM-POUNDS

2-BUTOXYETHANOL
SAY
TWO BEAU-TOX-EE-ETH-AN-OL

THESE CLEANING PRODUCTS POLLUTE IN TWO WAYS. THEY POLLUTE HUMAN BODIES WHEN THEY ARE USED, AND THEN POLLUTE THE ENVIRONMENT WHEN THEY ARE WASHED OR THROWN AWAY.

Carpet Cleaner
Toxin: Perchloroethylene or PERC. A **neurotoxin**. Can cause dizziness and loss of coordination.

Fabric Softener
Toxin: Quaternary ammonium compounds, or QUATS. Linked to asthma.

Oven Cleaner
Toxin: Sodium hydroxide. Extremely **corrosive**.

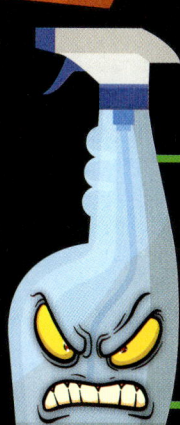

Window Cleaners
Toxin: 2-Butoxyethanol. Contributes to **necrosis**, **pulmonary oedema**, and severe liver and kidney damage.

Hand Soaps
Toxin: Triclosan. Can cause bacteria to become resistant to **antibiotics**, leading to **superbugs**! High levels found in rivers and streams.

IT'S IN THE WALLS!

FOR A WHILE, WE MANAGED TO CONVINCE THE HUMANS THAT ASBESTOS WAS A MIRACLE PRODUCT. THEY USED IT FOR ALL SORTS OF BUILDING PRODUCTS. IT IS MADE OF LOTS OF SMALL ...*SQUERGUZZZLE*... STRONG AND FLEXIBLE FIBRES. THE DUST THAT COMES OFF ASBESTOS, ESPECIALLY WHEN IT IS BROKEN, IS VERY BAD FOR HUMANS, BUT VERY GOOD FOR TOXLINGS.

THE DUST CONTAINS TINY FIBRES. THESE FIBRES LODGE THEMSELVES IN THE HUMANS' LUNGS AND STAY THERE FOREVER. IT COULD BE YEARS BEFORE THE EFFECTS ARE NOTICED.

UNFORTUNATELY, THE HUMANS GREW WISE TO THIS ONE AND STOPPED USING IT.

WHAT ABOUT THE LEAD PAINT? THAT WAS A GOOD ONE TOO.

OF COURSE, THE LEAD PAINT! HA HA ...*BLURP*... HA! BUT THEY CAUGHT ON TO THAT ONE TOO. YOU SEE, LEAD IS VERY TOXIC TO HUMANS AND THE ENVIRONMENT, BUT FOR A WHILE WE CONVINCED THE HUMANS TO PAINT THEIR WALLS WITH IT! HA HA ...*SPURTLE*... COUGH ...HA!

DANGER **LEAD HAZARD**
WORK AREA KEEP OUT
NO SMOKING, EATING, OR DRINKING

LEAD IS A TASTY TREAT ON OUR PLANET, BUT IT TURNS OUT THAT IT IS QUITE TOXIC TO HUMANS. IT CAN CAUSE NERVOUS SYSTEM DAMAGE, STUNTED GROWTH, KIDNEY DAMAGE AND DELAYED DEVELOPMENT.

FRAXULON AND ZURP'S TOP TOXIC TIPS
FOR TURMOIL

THE CASE OF THE TOXIC CATASTROPHE AT CORBY

TELL HER ABOUT CORBY!

AH YES – CORBY. IT IS JUST ONE EXAMPLE OF OUR MANY VICTORIES. YOU SEE, LOTS OF INDUSTRIAL MANUFACTURING ...*BLRUUUUP!*... CREATES INDUSTRIAL AND TOXIC WASTE. WHEN THE CORBY STEELWORKS IN THE UK CLOSED IN 1981, THEY NEEDED TO MOVE ALL THAT TOXIC WASTE.

CORBY
EAST NORTHAMPTONSHIRE
KETTERING
DAVENTRY
WELLINGBOROUGH
NORTHAMPTON
SOUTH NORTHAMPTONSHIRE

WELL, THE HUMANS WERE EVEN MORE CARELESS THAN WE COULD HAVE HOPED. THEY TRANSPORTED TOXIC WASTE ON OPEN TRUCKS STRAIGHT THROUGH THE TOWN, SLOSHING, SPLASHING AND SPILLING TOXIC WASTE ALL OVER THE PLACE.

Angelina was horrified to hear the aliens describe what this did to the babies that were born in Corby after the incident. She really didn't like these aliens at all!

THE VALLEY OF THE DRUMS AND THE LOVE CANAL

THEY TRIED TO CLEAN UP THE VALLEY OF THE DRUMS BUT THAT PLACE IS GOING TO BE TOXIC FOR EVER. OVER 100,000 DRUMS OF TOXIC WASTE WERE DELIVERED TO THE SITE BUT THEY ONLY BURIED 27,000. THE REST WERE JUST DUMPED IN DITCHES AND TRENCHES. THEY POLLUTED THE NEARBY CREEK.

IT IS STILL CONSIDERED ONE OF THE BEST HOLIDAY DESTINATIONS ON EARTH FOR A TOXLING.

EVEN BETTER IS THE LOVE CANAL: A SMALL TOWN NEAR NIAGARA FALLS WHICH WAS BUILT ON THE SITE OF A CHEMICAL DUMPING GROUND. YEARS LATER, TOXIC SLUDGE STARTED BUBBLING UP INTO PLAYGROUNDS, SCHOOLS, HOMES AND STREETS. THIS CAUSED AN INCREASE IN A TYPE OF CANCER CALLED LEUKAEMIA AND BIRTH DEFECTS AMONGST THE RESIDENTS.

Washington Montana North Dakota Minnesota Wisconsin Michigan New York New Hampshire Vermont Maine Massachusetts Rhode Island Connecticut Pennsylvania New Jersey Oregon Idaho Wyoming South Dakota Iowa Ohio Delaware Maryland Washington, D.C. Nebraska Illinois Indiana West Virginia Virginia Nevada Utah Colorado Kansas Missouri Kentucky North Carolina California Tennessee South Carolina Oklahoma Arkansas Alabama Georgia Arizona New Mexico Mississippi Texas Louisiana Florida

THANKS FOR THE MEMORIES

Now, devious as they are, Fraxulon and Zurp were so sure that victory was in hand – or, rather, in *tentacle* – that they had forgotten to search Angelina when they brought her aboard their ship. They did not know that all this time Angelina had been recording them on her phone.

Angelina was furious.

RECORDING

> YOU MONSTERS! I AM GOING TO TELL EVERYONE ABOUT YOUR TOXIC PLAN! THEN WE ARE GOING TO CLEAN THE PLANET UP AND KICK YOUR SLIMY TENTACLES OFF IT!

HA HA HA HA HA HA HA HA HA HA HA HA HA HA HA HA HA HA HA HA

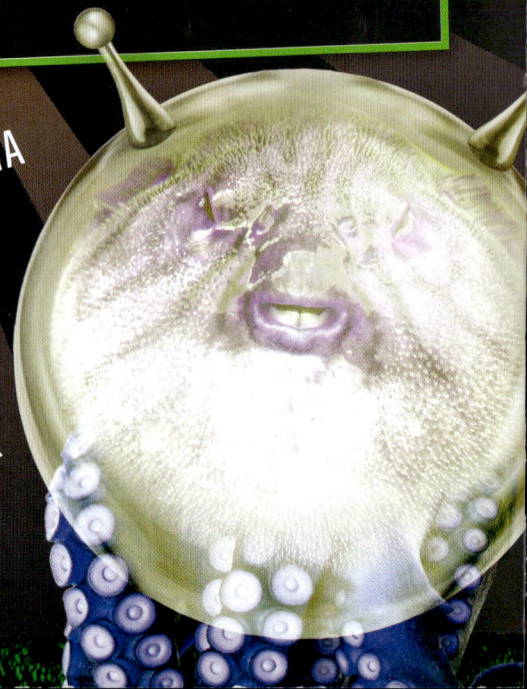

YOU WILL TELL NO ONE. WE ABDUCTED YOU BECAUSE YOU SAW US, BUT WE ONLY TOLD YOU OUR PLANS BECAUSE WE KNEW THAT YOU WOULDN'T REMEMBER. FRAXULON! READY THE UN-REMEMBERING DEVICE.

The device blasted our young hero with a bright light, and then everything went dark. Angelina woke up in the park with the worst headache she had ever felt and no memory of the last few hours.

But when Angelina checked her phone, she came across something strange. Something very strange indeed.

OOH, YOU LITTLE HUMANS COULDN'T GET ENOUGH OF THAT PLASTIC.

OF COURSE, THE LEAD PAINT! HA HA ...*BLURP*... HA. BUT THEY CAUGHT ON TO THAT ONE TOO. YOU SEE, LEAD IS VERY TOXIC TO HUMANS AND THE ENVIRONMENT.

OUR GREATEST TRICK WAS TO CONVINCE HUMANITY THAT IT COULD CREATE A SOLUTION TO ANY PROBLEM IN A LABORATORY.

EXPOSING THE CONSPIRACY

With the recording in hand, Angelina ran straight off to Number 10 Downing Street. She showed the Prime Minister the recording and explained that something must be done.

A global conference of world leaders was called. Soon, those who had been helping the Toxlings were identified and led away in handcuffs.

Breaking news. A young girl from the UK has uncovered a global conspiracy involving world leaders, heads of industry and... I'm sorry Bob, is this correct? Ahem... it has just been confirmed that, yes, a global conspiracy involving world leaders, heads of industry and ... ahem... aliens has been uncovered.

NEWS

Angelina was asked to hold a press conference in which she told the people of the world what had happened and what must happen next.

THE TOXLINGS ALMOST HAD US. THEY EXPLOITED OUR GREED AND IGNORANCE TO MAKE US THE TOOLS OF OUR OWN DESTRUCTION. WELL, NO MORE! WE MUST ALL TAKE RESPONSIBILITY FOR THE WORLD WE LIVE IN. WE MUST ALL WORK TOGETHER TO MAKE THIS WORLD CLEAN AND NATURAL AGAIN.

WHAT DID THE TOXLINGS DO SO WELL? THEY CHANGED OUR ATTITUDES AND HABITS. THAT IS WHAT WE MUST DO FOR OURSELVES NOW.

TOGETHER WE CAN CLEAN UP OUR HOMES AND OUR TOWNS, OUR INDUSTRIES AND OUR WORLD. WE WILL LEARN FROM OUR MISTAKES AND PROTECT THE ONE WORLD WE HAVE. NO MORE TOXIC WASTE. NO MORE TOXLINGS!

THE BIG CLEAN-UP

Angelina's words were heard around the world. Together, forgetting nationality, race or religion, the people of the world joined together to undo what had been done by the toxic aliens from outer space. New laws were put into place to stop manufacturing that resulted in unnecessary waste.

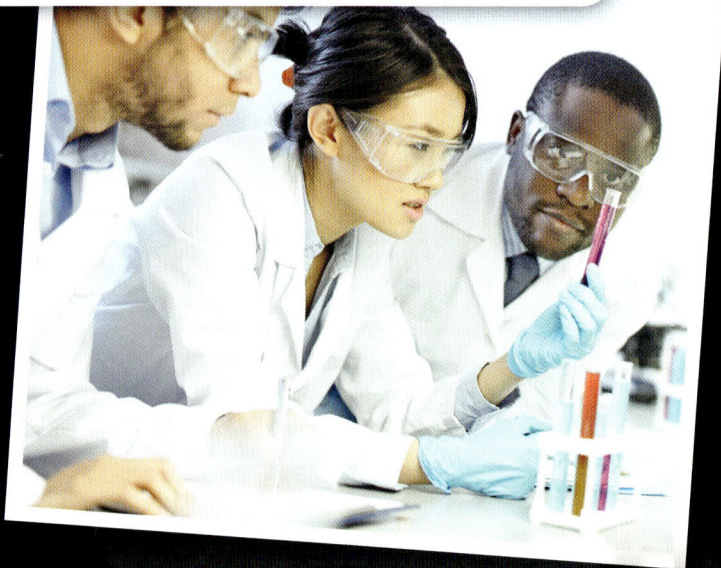

Scientists devoted themselves to finding ways to remove toxic waste from the environment.

The whole world joined together in the biggest litter pick ever seen. They removed almost all of the toxic, plastic litter from the oceans, towns and fields.

Only **renewable** and **sustainable** energy sources were used from that point on: no more toxic nuclear waste and no more harmful gases from fossil fuels.

Farmers only used natural ways to keep pests from their crops, instead of all those chemical pesticides.

These changes were by no means easy. Many people struggled to adapt to a new non-toxic lifestyle. But if anyone was tempted to use toxins again, they would simply ask themselves: 'What would Angelina do?'

Once the clean-up began, the Toxlings were never seen or heard from again.

NOOOOOOOO! ALL THAT BEAUTIFUL TOXIC WASTE GOING TO... WASTE! LET'S GET OUT OF HERE BEFORE THEY TRY AND CLEAN US UP TOO!

KEEP YOUR EYES
ON THE SKIES

And that, readers, is how a young girl from a small town saved the world from a toxic terror from outer space. Angelina still keeps a close eye on the skies, just in case the Toxlings are ever stupid enough to come back to Earth to try again.

But we mustn't forget the most important thing. The Toxlings may have given us the means to pollute our planet, by placing plastic, oil and other terrible things there for us to use, but it was always our decision to use them. So goodnight, dear reader, and may your dreams be sweet and unpolluted.

GLOSSARY

21ST CENTURY — the period of time beginning on the 1st of January 2001 and ending on the 31st of December 2100

ANTIBIOTICS — a medicine that destroys or stops the growth of micro-organisms

BIODEGRADE — broken down by natural organisms such as bacteria

CORROSIVE — capable of wearing down a material, usually through a chemical reaction

DEVELOPING ECONOMIES — countries with trade and monetary systems that have been weak but are now growing and becoming stronger

EXPLOIT — take advantage of

IGNORANCE — lack of knowledge or awareness

INDUSTRIAL REVOLUTION — a period of time from the late 1700s to the early 1800s when technology changed how things were made

INFILTRATED — to have moved into an organisation or country secretly without being detected

LANDFILLS — where waste is buried

LEACH — to draw chemicals out of an object, or to drain away from soil

MANIPULATING — cleverly controlling or influencing

MANUFACTURING — making large quantities of something

MUSTARD GAS — a chemical weapon used in the First World War that causes burns to the skin and irritation to the eyes and airways

NECROSIS — the death or rot of a piece of tissue

NEFARIOUS — wicked or evil

NEUROTOXIN — a toxin that affects the nervous system

OBSOLESCENCE — the process of becoming unnecessary or non-functioning

OIL REFINERIES — locations used to change crude oil into oil products such as petrol

PSYCHOLOGY — the study or knowledge of the human mind and behaviour

PUBERTY — when a child's body grows and changes to become more like an adult's body

PULMONARY OEDEMA — a build-up of fluid on the lungs

RENEWABLE — able to be replaced through natural processes

STUNTED — prevented from growing properly

SUPERBUGS — bacteria that has become resistant to antibiotics

SUSTAINABLE — able to be maintained at a certain rate or level

SYNTHETIC — man-made and not found in nature

UNINHABITABLE — a place where humans and animals are unable to live

INDEX